PARIS *in the Fifties*

PHOTOGRAPHS BY SANFORD ROTH

PARIS *in the Fifties*

Introduction by Aldous Huxley

Text by Beulah Roth

MERCURY HOUSE, *Incorporated*

San Francisco

Published in the United States
by Mercury House
San Francisco, California

Distributed to the trade
by Kampmann & Company, Inc.
New York, New York

Mercury House and colophon are registered trademarks
of Mercury House, Incorporated

Manufactured in the United States of America

Library of Congress Cataloging-in-Publication Data

Roth, Sanford, 1906–1962.
  Paris in the fifties.

  1. Paris (France)—Description—Views.   2. Paris
(France)—Social life and customs—20th century.
3. Roth, Sanford, 1906–1962—Journeys—France—Paris.
4. Roth, Beulah Spigelgass—Journeys—France—Paris.
5. Photography—France—Paris.   I. Roth, Beulah
Spigelgass.   II. Title.
DC707.R67   1988   779'.994436   88–5360
ISBN 0–916515–43–5

For my brother,
Leonard Spigelgass
(1908–1985),
who was the ultimate
Francophile

Acknowledgments

Merci beaucoup to Alev Lytle, executive editor of Mercury House, who thought about doing a book on Paris in the fifties long before it entered my mind. To Dorris Halsey, my dear friend and literary agent, who loves Paris as much as I do. To Carol Pitts and Carol Costello, Mercury House editors, who know how to decipher a writer's bad typing. To Sharon Smith, who designed this book with her God-given talents and her impeccable taste. To Zipporah Collins, whose mind can only be compared to the *Encyclopaedia Britannica*. Credit and thanks must be given to Joe Flowers of the La Peer Custom Lab in Los Angeles, who printed my husband's thirty-five-year-old negatives with tender loving care. To Monsieur De Latreppe, my French teacher at Erasmus Hall High School in Brooklyn, who introduced me to the joy of learning a second language, even though the subjunctive and the second person singular are still mysteries. Finally, my gratitude and eternal love to the city of Paris and all Parisians, for giving me the best years of my life.

Beulah Roth

Joe
Flowers
(213)
939
6756
or
6753
H

Contents

The French of PARIS

IT IS JUST FIFTY YEARS since I was in Paris for the first time, and all that remains to me of that childhood excursion is a memory of something which I am now inclined to believe I never saw and of something else which, at that time, was unmentionable in polite Anglo-Saxon society.

The thing I remember without having seen it—or did I see it?—was a gigantic tramcar, three stories high and driven by steam. Two-decker steam trams—these are antecedently probable, these I am prepared to accept. But what I remember, what I can still see with my mind's eye, is a green, puffing skyscraper on rails. Such a thing is beyond belief; but perhaps, none the less, it really existed. One of the greatest charms of this queer universe of ours, and one of its greatest horrors, is the actuality of the infinitely unlikely—the actuality, for example, of swallow-tail butterflies and the actuality of Adolf Hitler, the actuality of elephantiasis and Mongolian idiots and the actuality (as I still nostalgically hope) of three-story tramcars driven by steam.

Of the reality of those other things I so vividly remember, but was not allowed to talk about, there is no shadow of doubt. The things are there to this day, and Mr. Roth, in his picture of Place Pigalle, has given us irrefutable evidence of the fact. The Parisian *vespasienne* is Functional Architecture at its austere best. But, in 1901, what impressed the diminutive tourist was not the stark beauty of the design, but the conspicuousness and the ubiquity of the unspeakable object. There seemed to be a public convenience at practically every corner. On the infant Anglo-Saxon the impact of this particular aspect of Parisian life was powerful in exact proportion to the elaboration and rigidity of the Late-Victorian code of manners. In London the comfort stations were all safely below ground, hidden away like repressed memories of a disgraceful action. But, oddly enough, when you descended into one of these emblems of a guilty conscience, you found a positively Neronian splendour of marble, of porcelain, of copper piping, of mosaic floors, of crystal cisterns automatically discharging themselves five times an hour. And in many of those cisterns, as I remember, a nature-loving Borough Council had placed gold-fish. Theirs, poor things, was a nightmarish existence. Punctually every twelve minutes, their universe would start to rush down the drain. As the water level sank, the terror mounted. There was a frenzied darting to and fro, a panic flapping of fins and tails. And then, within half an inch of the Last Judgment, the drain would close as inexplicably as it had opened. Hissing and bubbling, life flowed back into the fishes' dying world. For a fifth of an hour there was peace and precarious, apprehensive happiness. Then, with a diluvian roar, yet another Golden Age was over, yet another Time of

And Frenssh she spak ful faire and fetisly
After the scole of Stratford atte Bowe,
For Frenssh of Parys was to hire unknowe.

CHAUCER
PROLOGUE TO
THE CANTERBURY TALES

INTRODUCTION BY ALDOUS HUXLEY

Troubles had begun. I did not know it at the time; but what I was watching there, underground, was an animated cartoon of human history.

In Paris, at the street corners, there were none of London's secret amenities. The functionalism was without trimmings, uncompromising, absolute. "Man," the *vespasiennes* mutely proclaimed, "man is merely the highest of animals. All pretensions abandon, ye who enter here!" To the heir of two generations of Victorian make-believe, this Gallic realism was at once appalling and exhilarating.

Children do most of their living either in phantasy, or in the timeless present. For them, as for the late Henry Ford, history is bunk. No, not even bunk—just non-existent. I must have done the museums with the rest of my family, I must have visited Notre-Dame and the Sainte Chapelle and the Palace of Versailles; but nothing remains to me of all this sightseeing. The Paris of my earliest recollections consists only of the things that evoked my childish wonder—*vespasiennes* and three-decker tramcars. It was not until several

years later that I began to be aware of Paris as a city of monuments, Paris as the embodied summary of European history. How many sermons in its stones! What books in its fountains and its muddy river! Consider, for example, the matter of vistas. Paris, as every tourist knows, is a city of vistas. From the windows of the Louvre you look up the Champs-Élysées, through two miles of geometrical and atmospheric perspective, to the Arc de Triomphe; and this same Arc de Triomphe stands at the vanishing point of eleven other prospects, only a little less grandiose than the first. Then there is the vista from the Place de la Concorde down the whole length of the Tuileries Gardens. The vista up the rue Royale to the Madeleine. The vistas which end in the Invalides and the Observatory. The upward vistas, from a thousand noisy intersections, of the balloon-like domes of the Sacré-Coeur. The vast and preposterous vista that links the Palais de Chaillot, through the straddling legs of the Eiffel Tower, with the École Militaire. (This last vista was still more charmingly absurd in the good old days, before the conventionally 'modern' Palais de Chaillot had replaced the Trocadéro. That earlier conjunction of Mid-Victorian phantasy, Late-Victorian technology and eighteenth-century classicism was unforgettably odd.) Historically, these Parisian vistas have one thing in common; they are all relatively recent. The earliest of them dates from the time of the absolute monarchy; the most grandiose are Napoleonic. Before the seventeenth-century—before Henry IV and Richelieu and Mazarin—nobody was interested in vistas. The fact that, from certain points on the embankment of the Seine, one can see Notre-Dame at a distance of a mile or more is due, not to human design, but to an accident of nature. One cannot build houses on a river. That is why there are vistas ending in Notre-Dame. Like most of the Greek

temples before them, most Gothic churches were built where it was impossible to see them as architectural wholes. Within the circuit of their walls, ancient and mediaeval cities were horribly overcrowded. There was no room for vistas. There was also—and this is more important—no interest in vistas. For ancient Greeks and mediaeval Europeans, the important thing about a temple or a church was its sacredness, not its appearance. What they wanted primarily was a religious, not an aesthetic, emotion. There is, of course, a 'beauty of holiness'; but there is also a holiness without beauty, or at least without conscious attention to beauty. At one end of the spiritual scale we find the primitively superstitious, kneeling before sacred objects possessed, in all too many cases, of no aesthetic value whatever; at the other end stand the mystics, for whom infinity and eternity are present at every point of space-time, the ridiculous no less than the sublime. The Paris of the vistas was created by secularist governments. Nominally Christian, the religion of these governments was actually an idolatory of the national state, and their purpose in cutting these theatrically grandiose vistas was to astound the public into believing

that a man-made organization was somehow divine. The most super-colossal of the French capital's permanent movie sets was designed by Napoleon. This was only to be expected. The usurper, the military dictator could not rely on the time-hallowed loyalties which had shored up the legitimate monarchy. The old kings had ruled by a right which was regarded as divine. In order to fabricate a divinity of his own, the parvenu Emperor resorted to all the tricks of the theatre and the motion picture studio. Out-Reinhardting Max Reinhardt, out-Cecilling B. de Mille, he dedicated the Arc de Triomphe and its system of vistas to the greater glory of himself, his army and France. To the philosophical eye, the Étoile is not merely a splendidly effective piece of town-planning; it is also the most perfect symbol of that nationalistic idolatry which has replaced Christianity and Judaism, Islam and Buddhism and Hinduism, as the effective religion of modern man. The Étoile is what the Indians call a *mandala*—a symbolic diagram that expresses or suggests the nature of cosmic reality. In Indian *mandalas* the design radiates out from a central area, which is always empty. This signifies that the divine Reality underlying appearances is beyond our understanding and cannot be expressed except in negative terms as neither this nor that. In the Napoleonic *mandala* the central reality is not the Void, which symbolizes the immanent and transcendent Spirit; it is the Arc de Triomphe. The god we are invited to worship is not God, but the State, the armed and aggressive Nation.

But happily there is much more in Paris than Napoleonic vistas and symbols of nationalistic idolatry. There are charming little country houses completely surrounded by modern business. There are whole quarters which look like the capital of some quiet subprefecture in Burgundy or Poitou. There are ancient streets, originally laid out for pack horses and pedestrians, and incompatible not merely with the automobile, but even with that new-fangled invention, the carriage and pair. In a score of brilliant and often amusing photographs, Mr. Roth has expressed the very spirit of these islands of provincialism, these deposits of fossil history. He shows us a life that continues to be lived, in spite of two World Wars, very much as it was lived in the days of President Loubet. The artisan is not extinct, and commerce is still predominantly an affair of small-scale shop-keeping. The customer is not confronted across the counter by the representative of a giant corporation. He is a person dealing with independent persons—with persons and, in very many cases, with their pets. Minou purrs among the vegetables or bottles, Médor dozes by the door, or trots out to smell the news of passing friends and leave a visiting card of his own.

These dealings of persons with persons are made smooth by the lubricant of a formal politeness. There are two ways of showing that one is a democrat. In America the cowhand addresses his millionaire boss as Joe or Charlie. In France the fourteenth Duke addresses his concierge as *Madame.* Both ways are good, and of both it is possible to grow a little tired. Too much protocol can be a bore. But so can too much familiarity from strangers, too much backslappng and first-name calling by half-baked adolescents. In France one sometimes pines for the Far, the Free and Easy West. And in the West one sometimes pines for the impersonal *Monsieurs* and *Madames* of the other democratic tradition.

As a child, as a schoolboy, I knew only the physical appearance of Paris and the Parisians. But as my knowledge of French increased, I became aware of other, less immediately obvious aspects of the city. By the time I was eighteeen I had developed a

passion for French literature. But literature implies books, and books imply bookshops, and in Paris there are more bookshops to the square mile than in any other city with which I am acquainted.

These bookshops! What an immense profusion! And what a blessed cheapness! In those early days there were reprints of practically everything at ninety-five centimes. And even the latest novel or volume of essays cost only three francs fifty. Except for collectors' items—and I never felt the desire or had the money to become a collector— the price of second-hand books was no less reasonable. In their brown calfskin, if they were of the seventeenth or eighteenth century, in paper or in mottled boards, if they had been published after 1820, they stood there in the deliciously smelly twilight, shelf above shelf, from floor to ceiling. Those dim caverns of forgotten literature, of dead philosophy and superannuated science were earthly paradises. And when their darkness became a little oppressive, there were always the open-air markets on the Quais. Half a mile of books and old engravings, with the river immediately behind and below them, and the Louvre rising majestically in the background. Could one ask, could one reasonably hope, for anything better?

Then came the Deluge. When the tide of blood had withdrawn, when, in 1919, it became possible once more to travel on the continent, the franc was a thing of paper, worth only a fifth of its gold-based predecessor. But the bookstalls along the river, the second-hand shops around Saint-Sulpice, the huge emporium under the arcades of the Odéon, the specialists in erudition of the Boulevard Saint-Michel—they were all there, as though nothing had happened. They are still there, thank heaven!—but under increasing difficulties. The costs of production go up faster than do the incomes of book-lovers. In France, as in every other country, it is becoming more and more difficult to publish a worst-seller or a highbrow magazine. The direct censorship of the totalitarian states has its counterpart, among the democracies, in the indirect censorship of mounting costs. In the fields of literature and learning, of critical journalism, of the theatre and the cinema, this new democratic censorship is making steady and insidious headway. In a few years it should work almost as effectively as the dictators' system of licensing before publication and (if heresy should still rear its ugly head) of shooting and forced labour afterwards.

Meanwhile, though the economic handicaps are daily increasing, a torrent of new volumes still continues to pour from the presses of France. The bookshops, hundreds and thousands of them, are still in business. And they are in business not merely in Paris, but throughout the provinces, in the most somnolent of market towns, the dreariest of industrial cities. Travelling through the United States, I have found myself in cities of as many as forty or fifty thousand inhabitants where it was impossible to buy a book. The local drug store and newsstands carried only pulp magazines and twenty-five-cent murder mysteries. Any other kind of literature was simply unobtainable. In France,

astonishing as it may seem, you can buy André Gide at most railway stations and Paul Valéry practically everywhere.

Even before 1914 I knew something of French books and of the places where they were sold. But it was not until after the war that I began to know some of the makers of those books. Paris now became, as well as everything else, a place where one met people whose interests were the same as one's own, and talked literary shop. But, in France at least, one cannot talk literary shop without sitting in cafés. Founded for the encouragement, impartially, of alcoholism and good conversation, of political discussion and idleness, of extra-conjugal love and the development, through impassioned dialectic, of new theories of ethics, aesthetics and metaphysics—the Parisian café is one of those institutions whose appeal is universal. It is for all tastes and for all purposes. My own tastes and purposes are mainly literary and, over the years, I have indulged the one and fulfilled the other at iron tables all over Paris. In 1920 the meeting place was generally a little café in the Passage du Panorama. Then it moved to Montparnasse, then to the Chez Francis, near the Pont de l'Alma—the setting chosen by Jean Giraudoux for

one of the acts of his *La Folle de Chaillot*. More recently it has shifted to Saint-Germain des Prés, where the Café des Deux Magots and the Café de Flore, on one side of the Boulevard, confront the Royal Saint-Germain on the other. Across all these table-tops, over innumerable cups of coffee and glasses of vermouth and soda, the talk reverberated back and forth. Talk, in those earliest days of my acquaintance with Parisian talkers, about Cubism (then only some ten years old) and about Dadaism (which was brand new and most satisfyingly iconoclastic). A little later one talked about the successive volumes of Proust's enormous novel—so fascinating then, but now, on a re-reading in another context and by a different 'me', so curiously unsatisfying. And then there was talk about Paul Valéry—or, much better, talk *with* Paul Valéry; talk which, for a foreigner, was no less fatiguing than rewarding; for Valéry spoke faster than anyone I have ever listened to and with an indistinctness of utterance most unusual in a Frenchman. His conversation was like that of an oracle—marvellous but enigmatic, illuminating but not entirely comprehensible. The thirties saw the rise of Surrealism. The German Romantics came into fashion; Lautréamont was hailed as the greatest of French authors. It was the best of fun. But unfortunately the real has a most unpleasant way of eclipsing the super-real, and the real, at that particular moment of history, was Fascism, was Marxist theory and Communist practice. The talk about these things was as lively as the talk about Surrealism. But, unfortunately for everyone concerned, French politics have tended, for some time now, to be more brilliant in theory than in practice. The conversations about statecraft were first-rate; the governments of the Third Republic were not. What was the reason for this melancholy state of affairs? The answer is to be found, by

implication, in Mr. Roth's admirable photograph of the statue of Henri IV. He sits there, the *Vert Galant*, mutely reminding the deputies, as they go in and out of the Chamber, that even in France good, strong government is not impossible. Not impossible—but, oh, how difficult! Just how difficult the plaque attached to the pedestal of good King Henry's statue plainly reveals. DÉFENSE D'URINER. We read and suddenly, in a flash, we understand the whole problem. French governments find it so hard to rule, because French citizens believe so passionately, so intransigently, in individual liberty. Thus, Paris is full of *vespasiennes;* but if a descendant of the men who stormed the Bastille should feel inclined to make use of the base of the statue of France's best king, he can see no valid reason for refraining. True, the Collective Will forbids, and the cops are on hand to enforce the prohibition. But let the cops turn their backs for even a moment: the descendant of the men who stormed the Bastille claims his inalienable right to do as he damn well pleases. Liberty triumphs over public spirit, and triumphs not merely in this little matter of committing a nuisance, but also in such far graver matters as black-marketeering and cheating the tax collector. There can be too much even of a very good thing. One of these days too much individualism may bring a dictator to the Élysée Palace. The very thought of such a thing is unutterably horrible; but for that very reason it has to be entertained, bitterly ruminated and, let us hope, sensibly and appropriately acted upon. King Henry's statue and the inscription on its pedestal are worth a whole treatise on politics. Tempering excessive individualism, public spirit will have to make that cop-enforced prohibition unnecessary. When that happens, and only when that happens, French democracy will find itself at once effective and secure.

Aldous Huxley
1953

This was PARIS

I AM A PASSIONATE FRANCOPHILE, a self-adopted Parisienne. My love affair with Paris began long ago when I was a teenager on my first trip abroad. The year was 1927, and our boatload of American students arrived in France exactly two months after Charles Lindbergh had crossed the Atlantic in the *Spirit of St. Louis* and landed at Le Bourget. The French embraced us, symbolically and physically, as they did everyone who carried the green American passport. Lindbergh had made us the darlings of the world. Paris seemed to be carpeted in welcome mats. Oh, how they loved us! Until August, that is.

In August, all their love and respect for the stars and stripes turned to hatred. Two gentlemen named Sacco and Vanzetti replaced Lindbergh in French hearts and reversed the French attitude toward Americans. Socialists around the world protested that these Italian immigrants had not been given a fair trial in the United States and were being executed more for their radical anarchist beliefs than for the murder of which they were accused. The French joined wholeheartedly in the demonstrations.

Being politically unaware at the time, I was confused. I knew that France and America were eternal friends. History books told us about Lafayette and his contribution to our Revolution. Our doughboys had fought shoulder to shoulder with the French *poilus* in World War I. Now, suddenly, Americans were persona non grata in France. To the French, nothing could excuse the injustice of the Sacco-Vanzetti executions. Difficult as this change in attitude was for me, it actually gave me an insight into the French character. I fell in love with the French people because of their convictions. I had witnessed *"Liberté, Égalité, et Fraternité"* in action.

Josephine Baker sang, *"J'ai deux amours, mon pays et Paris"* (I have two loves, my native land and Paris). I still love my native Brooklyn, despite the destruction of its many landmarks. Brooklyn remains a Utopia, if only in the caverns of my memory.

My other love, of course, is Paris. Not the cliché Paris of the Folies Bergère, the Moulin Rouge, the Lido, the four-star restaurants, the grand boulevards, the famous names of haute couture, and the renowned vintage wines. Underneath all that glitter and glamour lies the real Paris, the Paris of the people—lower-, middle-, and upper-class citizens, blue-collar workers, intellectuals, and even *clochards* (street people). There must be "fifty million Frenchmen" (to quote a song of the day) who have never been to the Folies Bergère or patronized those palaces of leather handbags and silk scarves, Gucci and Hermès. But those "fifty million Frenchmen" buy their fresh baguettes twice a day and scour regional flea markets for bargains.

My husband and I became expatriates the day we arrived in Paris in 1947. Sandy had decided to give up a promising career in business to pursue his real passion, photography. Where better than in postwar Paris?

Paris was a shambles then, trying to recover from the humiliation of the German occupation.

PARIS 6
1955

Strict rationing was in force, and the game that year was to identify those Parisians who had collaborated with the Germans. The political divisions were clear: You had been a collaborationist or you hadn't. Many Parisians had escaped to safer environments during the occupation; others had remained and managed to live fairly normal lives under the Germans. And there were countless stories of people who had become resistance fighters in their own small ways. A milliner in Montparnasse had used her shop window to flaunt the colors of the French flag—blue, white, and red—in a changing display of hats, with perhaps a red umbrella, white gloves, or a blue handbag. It was her daring attempt to defy *"les Épinards,"* Parisian slang for the German soldiers, who wore spinach-green uniforms.

I recall, too, a stylish, elegant nightclub in Paris, Le Monseigneur, that had twenty-nine violinists, all of them former members of symphony orchestras who had escaped from Nazi-occupied cities to Paris. Chatting at the end of one evening, after Le Monseigneur had closed, they told me that all through the occupation, when the nightclub was filled with German officers, they had played the music of freedom fighters—especially the songs sung by the Spanish Republicans during

their civil war. The Germans were too saturated with champagne to recognize what they were hearing. I doubt if they listened, so involved were they with the *belles poitrines* of their *compagnons* of the evening. Their tongues were loose, too, and many a secret military movement was relayed to the Resistance within minutes.

I also heard about a canine Resistance hero named Azore, a Belgian shepherd who wore a rather intricate collar. Azore's mistress was the *directrice* of a well-known fashion house that catered to the often outrageous tastes of the German officers' wives and mistresses. The gossip in her salon sometimes revealed military secrets. Madame X wrote down all the information on a small piece of paper and inserted it into Azore's collar. Then she commanded, "Azore, go to Jean!" Azore ran up Avenue George V, crossed the Pont de l'Alma, and delivered the note to Jean, somewhere on the Left Bank.

The fifties in postwar Paris were an **American's** dream come true. The franc was legally valued at about 400 to the dollar. But, if you had a private money changer who dealt on the black market, you might get 600 or 700 francs for your greenback. Our money changer was a woman, Madame S, and her telephone calls to us were so shrouded in coded information that we often lost out on great moments in the history of the exchange rate. I became an expert in arbitrage: I would buy $200 worth of French francs with American dollars, then use the francs to buy pounds sterling, which I exchanged in turn for Swiss francs. Sometimes I could turn a profit of about 30 percent from all this currency shopping. So important was the black market that the Paris *Herald Tribune* published the black market rates along with the legal rates every day.

Then as now, restaurants were obliged to display their menus and prices in a place visible to potential diners. We judged how expensive a restaurant would be by the price of only one item on the menu —*foie de veau* (calf's liver). If it cost 400 francs ($1) or less, we entered. Fancier places such as the Tour d'Argent might ask twice as much, the extravagant price of $2.

We were shocked to learn that double rooms at *grand luxe* hotels such as the Ritz or the George V went for $20 a day. We were paying the equivalent of $3 a day in a very adequate hotel, the Lutèce, in Montparnasse—and our room even had a *bath*.

How times have changed! Recently I was in Paris and stayed at a *grand luxe* hotel, the Bristol. I have to say that it was absolutely magnificent. My room had curtains and a bedspread of blue silk taffeta. The bath was pink marble with Porthault towels and after-bath robe. But, at $150 a day, it did not compare favorably to the Lutèce.

How much more fun living in Paris was then! At Dominique's, the Russian restaurant on our corner, the chefs practically force-fed every stray cat in the neighborhood on beef Stroganoff with sour cream. We had the Coupole, the Dôme, the Deux Magots, and the Flore just a few blocks away. There were always good friends on the terraces of these cafés, and the conversation was bright. We talked art, politics, fashion, and extraordinary gossip about friends who were not present.

The Hotel Lutèce was our art deco palace, with its Edgar Brandt bronze doors and room furnishings that had been the rage in 1927 (but were not too well preserved). It attracted an interesting clientele. First, there were the intellectuals who could afford a deluxe hotel but preferred to be in Montparnasse, the heart of the art and literary world. Then there were students like our neighbor in the next room, who was living on the GI Bill and had practically no money. Often when I passed his room and the door was slightly ajar, I noticed that his laundry was hung to dry on wires strung across the room. The management of the Lutèce had warned everyone, both verbally and in writing, that no drip-dry washing would be tolerated. This was the age of drip-dry shirts, suits, underwear, and what have you. The drip from the drying caused mysterious leaks to the floor below, but our friend never seemed to get caught. Perhaps the management realized that his only alternatives were dripping dry or not washing at all.

The other clients of our hotel were the *putains* (prostitutes), whose field of action was the corner of Rue Jules Chaplain and Rue Brea. The nearest hotel was, of course, the Lutèce. Among these ladies, whom I liked very much despite their taste in clothes, was a girl with bright red hair and a false leopard coat. Both the hair and the coat made her more obvious than the other girls and, I suppose, a clearer target for the "*jeans.*" One night she came into the lobby of the Lutèce with a "gentleman." I happened to be waiting for my friend Aline Mosby, who was going to spend a few days with me in Paris before leaving for her U. P. I. post in Moscow. The little lobby was usually deserted at midnight, but there I was, seated on one of the worn leather chairs, in my bathrobe. (One could do this at the Lutèce, but surely not at the George V.) When my red-haired neighbor saw me, she was embarrassed and spoke to the concierge as though she wanted to engage a room for the night after traveling all day. The young man on duty went along with this ridiculous charade being played for my benefit.

"Have you any luggage?" he asked.

Luggage? She had the customary baggage of the *putain,* a large handbag known to one and all as a *"cinq à sept."*

"Madame and Monsieur, did you want a double or single room?"

Because of me, the poor woman was deprived of her regular boudoir. As a rule, the Lutèce rented rooms for *"un petit moment"* and never inquired about luggage or passport.

The Lutèce had a chambermaid who was quite old and not really capable of doing the work the hotel demanded. When Aline came to visit, there was no room with a bath available at the Lutèce, and, since my husband was away in Rome, I invited Aline to share my room. The large double bed provided both of us with a comfortable and much needed sleep. In the morning, I rang for breakfast—the usual coffee, croissants, butter, and jam. Ten minutes later, there was a knock on the door. But, instead of waiting for me to say *"Entrez,"* the aging chambermaid breezed in with her usual greeting, *"Bonjour, Monsieur, Madame!"* Seeing two women in bed, she dropped the tray and ran off in shock, blushing to the roots of her white hair. Although she had served prostitutes and their companions for years, the sight of Aline and me so outraged her sense of propriety that none of my explanations had any effect on her.

Among the greatest amusements Sandy and I enjoyed—with thousands of Parisians, interior decorators, and collectors from all over the world—were the Sunday trips to the flea markets. The best known was and still is the Marché Biron in Clignancourt, a working-class district of Paris. The small stalls were filled with treasures of another era. We never knew what we would find. It might be an eighteenth-century chair or table, a Gallé glass vase, a Toulouse-Lautrec drawing, or a ball gown that had once belonged to Sarah Bernhardt. The art of browsing reached its apogee as we strolled through the maze of stalls and alleys. Behind the Biron were other markets, secret ones hidden from the tourist who lacked a spirit of adventure.

Knowing how to bargain was usually an acquired talent for Americans. Europeans had done it for centuries and wouldn't think of buying anything for the asking price. It wasn't done, of course, in department stores and boutiques—but sometimes I wondered about that. My instruction in flea market bargaining came from a Greek friend who was a past master in the art. You begin, he advised, by choosing an object and asking the price. Even if the price is low, you don't accept it. You walk away. Not too far, he cautioned, just far enough to make the vendor regret his loss of a customer. In a

moment, you should hear him call, "Madame!" As you casually return to his stall, he asks, "How much will you pay?" At this point you name a ridiculously low figure—half of the asking price. He turns his back on you, but only for a minute. Now he is ready to compromise. He names a price. You say "no" and walk away again. At this point, he calls you back and, with a desperate shrug of his shoulders, agrees to your offer. Personally, I find it uncomfortable to go through this routine. But I have been told that it is expected. It takes the boredom out of antique shopping and gives the dealer his amusement for the day.

I still think of those glorious days in January when I would open *Le Figaro* and see, hidden away on page four, a small advertisement headed by the word *"Solde."* That word "Sale" was magic enough, but when I read that the sale was at Schiaparelli or Rochas or Hermès, it was almost too much for a red-blooded American bargain hunter to bear.

At eight o'clock one January morning, my husband and I rushed over to Place Vendôme. Schiaparelli's doors were still closed, but a line already stretched around the corner on Rue de la Paix. We waited and waited for the opening rush. Suddenly an old man standing in front of us turned and asked if this was the line for the distribution of chocolate or biscuits or perhaps butter. I explained that it certainly was not, it was for expensive dresses and accessories. The old man was quite crestfallen and announced his disappointment loudly, using a five-letter word appropriate to the occasion. At once, half of the people in line left, putting us two steps from Schiaparelli's door.

That day, I selected from the feast of Schiaparelli's leftovers a pair of ocelot boots trimmed in patent leather for seven dollars, three sweaters for two dollars each, a marvelous hat trimmed with ivy leaves in shades of green lace for four dollars, and

a handbag that I still use (it has become quite the conversation piece).

During the few days Aline Mosby was in Paris, we shared a great adventure. One cold Sunday morning in January, we went to the flea market. Strolling through the alleys, I recognized a couple from Hollywood. Sam Marx, an executive at MGM, and his wife had never met me, but I knew who they were. As they passed, I said, *"Bonjour, Monsieur Marx."*

He looked at me with surprise, and his wife stared with suspicion.

"Who is that?" she must have asked him. I didn't catch his reply and didn't want to start any domestic upheavals, so Aline and I walked on. Five minutes later, we encountered them again.

"Mr. Marx," I said, in English this time, "my name is Beulah Roth, and I am Leonard Spigelgass's sister." (My brother was a Hollywood writer.)

"How nice to see you. What are you doing in Paris?"

"I live here, and I speak French. Is there anything I can help you with?"

Mr. Marx was so grateful that he insisted Aline and I come to the Ritz Hotel for a drink and dinner that evening. He added that his Aunt Blanche was married to the director of the Ritz, and he thought we should meet her.

Our meeting with Aunt Blanche was historic. She told us that she had come to France in the early twenties with her friend, Pearl White, who had been a famous silent screen actress. Her greatest role had been in *The Perils of Pauline*, a serial film that had had my brother and me biting our fingernails while the heroine, Pauline, lay tied to a railroad track in the path of an oncoming train or endured the Chinese water torture. Pearl White had brought more people into movie theaters than John Barrymore.

Aunt Blanche was from Brooklyn, where she and Pearl White had become dear friends. One day they both decided to go to France and look for rich husbands. Pearl actually trapped one, but Blanche fell in love with a lowly hotel manager. As years passed, however, Blanche's charming husband became director of the Ritz and one of the most distinguished men in France. At dinner that night, he and I discovered that we shared a passion for cream of mushroom soup and wild strawberry tarts. Later, Aunt Blanche asked Aline and me, "Do you girls like Chanel clothes?"

What a question!

"You see," she continued, "Coco Chanel is my best friend, and I know when they are going to have a sale. Are you interested?"

Both Aline and I shrieked with delight.

"All right," said Blanche, "meet me at Chanel tomorrow morning at nine, and I will introduce you to a *vendeuse* who can take you to the basement, where all the clothes are being marked for the sale. Choose anything you like, and I will arrange the lowest prices possible."

This was a dream come true. How often had I imagined myself surrounded by Chanels that I could buy for practically nothing? Early the next morning, Aline and I met Blanche in front of Chanel's establishment on Rue Cambon. She took

us into the sanctum sanctorum and there assigned us to a *vendeuse* in a little black dress and lots of pearls. We were stunned by the racks and racks of Chanel dresses, suits, coats, blouses, skirts, and everything else, being gathered for the January sale. Aline took one side of the room and I took the other.

It was almost more than I could bear, but I managed to choose a very Chanel bright blue jersey dress and a rust-colored tweed suit trimmed with ratty red fox. Then I forced myself to stop until I heard what kind of discount Aunt Blanche could arrange. Aline had chosen a black-and-white tweed coat lined in gray jersey. It was the ultimate Chanel, and I regretted that I hadn't seen it first. But Aline needed that coat. She was wearing a white belted number that looked so out of place in Paris that I urged her to buy the tweed coat whatever the price.

In a half-hour, Aunt Blanche came down to see what we had chosen. "My dears, you will be getting these things for practically nothing. Leave it to me!"

We left it to Blanche and waited patiently for her news. After an interminable three minutes, she came back beaming with delight.

"Here's the breakdown: The blue dress I managed to get you for $900—what a bargain! The suit, you can have for $1,500! You are stealing them!"

I looked at the blue dress again and noticed some perspiration stains under the arms, some ripped seams. These discoveries gave me the courage to say no. Blanche was amazed that anyone in her right mind would let a little imperfection interfere with the buy of a lifetime. So, I was forced to reveal the truth.

"I can't afford it, Blanche. I've never spent that much for clothes in my life."

Blanche was clearly disappointed, and I was

too. As for Coco Chanel, wherever she is in that great atelier in the sky, I hope she has forgiven me for not buying something from her collection.

Aline was not leaving Chanel without that tweed coat. Blanche told her the price would be only $500 because the dress that matched the lining was missing.

I don't know where Aline summoned up the courage to say, "I'll give you $125 and not a cent more! Furthermore, I want my white coat put into a Chanel box. I want a Chanel label in the tweed coat. And that's my final offer!"

Well, Aline got the coat, the box, and the label, and went off to Moscow feeling as though she had outwitted the fashion cartel.

The adventure ended in Moscow five years later, when Aline realized one day that the coat was falling apart. It had only been basted together, but it had served her for five years in that condition. Aline gave it to her housekeeper, who must be even now the most stylish woman in town. The housekeeper got the coat, but not the Chanel label.

There was very little *prêt à porter* (ready-to-wear) in the early fifties. Either you had to depend on couture bargain sales or you had to have things made to order. Paris was peppered with small dressmaking establishments, usually boutiques with model designs that could be copied in your size. The fee was modest and the workmanship superb, but the fittings were a bore. If you ordered a suit, usually a Dior New Look, with a taped waistline and a gored skirt, you submitted to five fittings *(cinq essayages)*. A suit made with only two fittings would turn out to be a size too large—or worse, too small. The price varied with the number of fittings. Some dressmakers would work with your fabric; others were adamant that you use what they had in stock.

I can recall a very stylish black wool suit I had made after the Dior New Look was *démodé*. The jacket was still nipped in at the waist but the skirt was straight. The entire jacket was trimmed with black passementerie braid, which I bought for the dressmaker at the Galeries Lafayette, the largest department store in Paris. Every woman in Paris had to have a suit with passementerie braid that year, and it was hard to find.

That was also the year the electricity was shut off at certain times and places in Paris. It was on from seven to nine in the morning, so that people could have illumination, elevator service, and other electrical necessities. It was turned off during the afternoon and put on again later in the evening. My suit fittings were during hours without electricity, but all shops, cafés, and business establishments had kerosene lamps to be used in those periods. The dressmaker's apprentice held the kerosene lamp over me while I was being pinned and chalked. At one point, I was asked to hold the lamp above my head like the Statue of Liberty, while the apprentice searched for more pins. Only the genius of French dressmaking could have produced a wearable garment under these circumstances.

The most important social event of the fall-winter season in Paris was *Le Bal des Petits Lits Blancs* (the Ball of the Little White Beds), a formal dress charitable affair for a children's hospital. Sandy and I were invited by a friend who had enough francs to pay for the tickets. To be invited to this gala was exciting, but the problem of what to wear was worrisome. Sandy managed to borrow a prewar tuxedo from a fellow photographer, so he had to invest only in a new evening shirt, black tie, cuff links, and studs. I had only a black taffeta little nothing of a dress, and I simply could not appear in that.

"What are you going to wear?" I asked the friend who had invited us.

"I really don't know yet, but come with me to Jacques Fath, and we'll see what they have."

The salon of Jacques Fath, at the time the most noted of the young couturiers, was hardly the place for a photographer's wife to buy a ball gown, I told my friend. She then confided her secret.

"My dear, nobody pays for anything at Fath. You just borrow things for the night. You appear in a Fath dress and wrap, and someone invariably will say, '*Ma chère*, your gown is marvelous. Where did you get it?' Then you simply say the magic words, 'Jacques Fath.' It's the best advertising a couture house can get."

So, my friend and I were ushered to an upper floor of the Fath establishment, where a *vendeuse* let us choose from racks of ball gowns. There were the velvets, satins, brocades, and fantastic silks that brought the prices of these dresses to the level of the national debt. I chose a saffron yellow stiff satin with a matching wrap, my friend a pale blue brocaded velvet. The dresses were fitted, hems measured to our heights, and then we were taken to the accessory department. Shoes first. There

was a pair in silver, gold, and matching yellow satin in my size, 7½ B. Of course I took those. My friend, who wore a size 9, didn't have much choice but managed to get into a pair of silver sandals. Handbags too. An antique Persian brocade for me and a silver leather for her. Next gloves. Oh yes, one wore long white kid gloves to this ball. Then I was asked if I had jewels to wear. I said that I had a string of pearls.

"Just one string? No madame, for this dress I want at least seven strands."

So down to the jewelry department we went and there found the perfect necklace. It was false, but the ultimate degree of chic. Those pearls could have passed anywhere for the real thing, and they did.

I had never imagined that anything so remarkable could happen to me. Cinderella would have looked shabby by comparison when I was dressed for that ball. And when I looked around the room, I wondered how many of the spectacular ball gowns I saw were destined to be returned to Dior, Balenciaga, Schiaparelli, and Balmain the next day, as I returned mine to Jacques Fath. At least I was queen for a night!

Sandy captured the moods of Paris so beautifully that, looking at the photographs now, I can actually smell the perfume I used then, Piguet's "Visa." Along with "Miss Dior," it was the scent of the fifties. "Visa" had an audacity that announced my comings and goings. It would linger on a staircase for hours and proclaim my presence to anyone who cared. The trouble was, I was not the only one in Paris who considered "Visa" her signature. It didn't take long for me to realize that quite a few ladies of the evening (and afternoon) found that the sexy, musky odor of "Visa" had an unusual appeal to gentlemen. The gentlemen in question did not dare

Out of necessity and love, cats are an integral part of Parisian life. I've seen a cat nestled in a ball gown displayed in the Galeries Lafayette. Cats guard grocery stores, museums, small businesses, and private apartments from assault by rodents, who have no respect for personal belongings. A rat's palate cannot be classed as gourmet. Rats love peanuts, telephone wires, silk lingerie, and dog biscuits.

I had a friend living in Paris who considered cats suitable pets only for women or questionable males. A German shepherd or a Doberman pinscher was the necessary adjunct to his own manliness. Of course the inevitable happened: A mouse, or perhaps a rat, with a voracious appetite discovered his precious supply of camembert cheese, Ry Krisp sent from New York, and Carr's Water Biscuits imported from London.

"Bring Louis, your cat, over here to see what he can do," my friend pleaded.

"That is not the answer," I said, knowing Louis. "You must have a live-in cat to catch these food thieves in the act."

"A cat to live here with me? Out of the question!"

I suggested that he borrow a cat from a nearby grocer for a few days. A lot of people did this when

return to their wives because the telltale evidence of a rendezvous clung to their clothes. If the wife happened to use Yardley's "Lavender," there was bound to be a domestic upheaval. Piguet stopped making "Visa" a long time ago. I often wonder why.

My husband and I were passionate animal lovers. To us, an animal was anything that wasn't human. Dogs, cats, horses, lions, tigers, and snails were among our favorites. To love a snail may seem neurotic to those who enjoy eating them, but we thought of them only as oppressed little creatures who enjoyed chewing on rosebuds and geranium leaves. One day as we walked through Rue de Buci, we passed a market stall that specialized in *escargots* proclaimed to be the best garden variety in Paris. Sandy looked at me, I looked at him, and silently we embarked on a rescue mission. We bought a kilo of snails, all alive and seemingly happy to have found friends. We carried them gently to the Luxembourg Gardens and set them free among the hydrangeas. George Bernard Shaw once proclaimed that he didn't eat anything he could pet. Although one cannot easily pet a snail, neither can I understand how anybody can eat one.

they didn't have a mouse catcher of their own. My friend agreed and went with me to the grocery store on Rue du Cherche Midi. Since he was a good customer, they let him have their beautiful gray tabby female, Athene. For the first two days, Athene sat on his kitchen windowsill manicuring her nails, using the temporary litter box, and ignoring my friend and his problem.

"Cats are useless!" he moaned. "Two days, and nothing has happened. Another biscuit is gone, and my cheeses are ruined!"

"The reason, *cher ami*, is that the cat knows you don't like her," I told him. "You are merely tolerating her as an instrument of destruction. Take my advice and caress her, talk to her in terms of endearment, offer her some cream and a sardine. Be gracious to your house guest, and she will respond."

Sure enough, Athene responded, presenting my friend with an obese mouse. Thankfully he stroked her back and discovered that she was more attractive than all the Dobermans in the world. In fact, he fell madly in love, and by the next day had adopted one of Athene's kittens to share his bed and board for life.

Sandy and I loved living at the Lutèce, but all we had was a bedroom and a bath, which didn't really accommodate our luggage and camera paraphernalia. It was time, we decided, to find an apartment. For some urgent reason, we had to go to New York for a week or so, but, before we left, we asked a friend to try to find something suitable for us. In New York a cable arrived from our friend announcing that the ideal, the perfect, the most unbelievable apartment was ours as soon as we came back to Paris. He added the useless information that it was next to the house where the Three Musketeers had lived. He did not give us the useful informa-

tion that the apartment was not solely ours—only partly. The rest we were to share with Madame Camus, who would be very cooperative in letting us use her bathroom and kitchen. He also neglected to tell us that the flat was six flights up and that there was no elevator!

Madame Camus was charming and obliging. "My bathroom is yours. But the toilet is in your part of the apartment, and I must have access to it at all times." (The French divide personal needs into two rooms: The toilet is a separate little closet containing just the toilet bowl; the bathroom contains the tub, washbasin, the obligatory bidet.) Thus we were deprived of any privacy in "our" part of the apartment. And when I tried to use Madame Camus's bathroom one day, I discovered a mysterious red powdery dust permeating everything in sight. It had a slight aroma of anise, adhered to the waterline of the tub, and tinted the usually white washbasin a pandemonium pink. I wondered whether it would be polite to ask Madame Camus what this substance was, but she soon volunteered that she was manufacturing a tooth powder guaranteed to make teeth healthy and pearly white. It was a sort of cottage industry. I tried to use the sample she gave me, but my teeth seemed less like pearls than pigeon blood rubies.

Poor Madame Camus was a dear, but not dear enough to live with. We told her a white lie—well, an almost-white lie—that my husband could not walk up and down six flights of stairs four times a day because of his heart. I assured her that we would try to sublet the apartment as quickly as possible.

We placed an advertisement in the Paris *Herald Tribune:* "Splendid apartment near Luxembourg Gardens. Two rooms plus generous use of bath and kitchen to share with charming Frenchwoman. An opportunity to learn the language and the secrets of French cooking. Rent reasonable. Suitable for two young women. Call Madame Camus, Odéon 4789."

Two splendidly athletic young women who worked at the Swedish Embassy answered the advertisement and moved in as soon as we moved out, back to the Lutèce, which had begun to have the allure of Versailles. Madame Camus called to let us know that her new tenants were absolutely adorable. She became a mother hen, protecting the little chicks. She cooked for them, cleaned their rooms, and even did their laundry. The six flights of stairs meant absolutely nothing to these two Nordics, who had climbed mountains. Now their adopted grandmother, Madame Camus waited for them at the top of the stairs each night. At last she had something more in her life than her red tooth powder.

Traveling abroad was fairly rare in the late forties and early fifties. There seemed to be an underground information network that told perfect strangers, friends of friends of friends of ours, when we were sailing on the *Île de France* or the *Liberté*. Somehow, we were always asked to take something to someone somewhere in England or France. Once a well-known actor in New York pleaded with us to take a trunk full of clothes to his sister in London.

We had to refuse because we were not going to England. He sent me a bouquet of lilies of the valley for my "charming refusal." But I did take many things to many people: witch hazel, sculptures to be cast in Paris, Yuban coffee, baking soda, Epsom salts, and a number of other items some Parisians had learned to love and now found unobtainable.

The most surprising request came from a gentleman I did not know. He came to our New York hotel carrying a brown paper package held together with ordinary string.

"Please do me a great favor. I want you to bring this to Alice B. Toklas. It is something she has waited for all through the war. I know you will enjoy meeting her, and when you see the pleasure on her face when she opens this, you will have your reward!"

I didn't know how to ask about the contents. Was it a bomb? A kilo of marijuana? A live snake? The package was too light to contain books and too heavy to be a silk nightgown. I had to know what was in it, just in case a French customs agent did a spot check looking for contraband.

With a silly grin on his face, the gentleman shyly revealed the secret within the package. "It is her squirrel scarf and a box of cornflakes!"

I agreed to deliver the package to Miss Toklas, selfishly hoping that she would consent to have Sandy photograph her. That would be a coup!

I put the Toklas package in a small duffel bag where I kept my shoes and soiled laundry. It went through French customs easily and remained in the duffel bag for a long, long time—I am ashamed to say, four months. We were then staying at the Hôtel Powers on Rue François Premier in a strange apartment on the top floor. It was rather unrentable because it had two empty rooms where the kitchen and bathroom should have been. The management had improvised a bathroom for us with some primitive inconveniences. But the rent was cheap, and the Napoléon III flea market furnishings were ugly but amusing. We installed ourselves in ersatz luxury, with lots of armoires where we stored our luggage and the clothes we did not need. Alice B. Toklas's package found its way into an armoire and out of my memory.

One day, the concierge of the Powers called our apartment to say that a woman was in the lobby acting like a mad dog. She demanded to talk to us, not in person, but on the telephone.

"Please, Madame," he said, "please do something. This woman is making a scene!"

I took the phone and heard the voice of Alice B. Toklas. She called me a thief, a four-letter word, and a five-letter word. She threatened to have me arrested if her possessions were not sent down to the lobby immediately. Overcome by embarrassment, I found the package and had it brought to her. I can still hear her voice, shrill and outraged, slinging verbal darts at me. I was told that she left the lobby still cursing my stupidity for neglecting to make the delivery to her.

The concierge asked me later what the scandal was about. I don't think he knew who Miss Toklas was, nor did he think that an old squirrel scarf and a box of cornflakes warranted her behavior.

"Madame," he told me, "I thought you had stolen her emerald necklace!"

In the early fifties, we bought a Citroën. The postwar Citroën was a utility car with all the attributes of an army Jeep. It was an inexpensive, inconspicuous car, unnoticed on Paris streets. At one point, we took a French freighter from Le Havre directly to Los Angeles. Thirty-one days at sea—fascinating but also somewhat boring, since there were only four other passengers, and they were all from Guatemala. Our baggage consisted of our cat,

Louis, and our Citroën. The California Department of Motor Vehicles insisted that we register the Citroën on arrival and replace our TT license with California plates.

When we returned to Paris, we shipped the Citroën back to France via the Panama Canal, while we took the train and the *Liberté*. Weeks later we picked up the Citroën in Cherbourg and drove it to Paris. I know it was happy to be home again—and so were we. As we drove around Paris, we began to notice that we were being followed by another Citroën. Wherever we went, the other car was behind us. We made unscheduled right turns and left turns, but there it was on our trail. Sometimes weeks would pass without a sign of the other car, and then suddenly it would appear again. It was a mystery. Who was the driver? If it was someone who knew us, why didn't he or she ask us to stop? Was it the police? Was it someone planning a hold-up? One day we saw that the other driver was a woman. Evil thoughts came into my mind: Did my husband have a mistress who was about to accost him in public? No, that was not possible—I knew where he was every minute of the day. Or did I?

The mystery was solved about two years later, when again we shipped the Citroën to Los Angeles. One day we parked the car in front of a supermarket on Santa Monica Boulevard in Hollywood. Another car pulled up behind us and a woman ran toward us almost hysterical with joy.

"At last I've found you again!" she shouted. "I chased you all over Paris, because you had California plates on your car, and now I've found you in California! I wanted to know who you were when I lived in France, because I was homesick. My name is Deanna Durbin. Forgive me!"

Deanna Durbin starred in countless films at Universal Studios during the thirties and forties. She had a magnificent singing voice, and was quite a celebrity. That day she came home with us and, over a cup of tea, told us that she was married to a Frenchman and lived in Neauphle-le-Château, not far from Paris, but made periodic trips to the city. The sight of our California license plates had made her nostalgic for her Hollywood years, and she became determined to meet us. It was the same determination she used to reach the high C in an aria in *La Bohème*.

Like every other city, Paris has changed. Buildings are demolished, hotels appear in the most outlandish places, and a new city has arisen on the outskirts of Paris in what was once a flowering meadow. The two landmarks I miss most are the Gare Montparnasse, now replaced by a skyscraper, and Les Halles, the great wholesale market of Paris that supplied food for the entire city. Les Halles embodied a way of life.

For the film *Irma la Douce*, art director Alexander Trauner designed an exact duplication of Rue du Faubourg St. Denis, where Irma's prototypes sauntered casually up and down, hoping to enchant the gentlemen who worked in Les Halles.

My husband and I knew all of the ladies well. Whenever we drove through Rue St. Denis, we greeted each of the business girls with "*Bonjour, Lili. Bonjour, Bébé. Bonjour, Kiki.*" They all waved in recognition of the two unknown friends who treated them as neighbors. There was a fat one in white boots and a satin dress that zipped up the side from her knees to her throat. She always stood in front of a small hotel, ready for any customer who might need her services. These ladies seemed to like each other. There was no rivalry or trespassing on another's territory. I suppose each had a specialty. I'm sure they gossiped about food and inflation. As far as I know, these women were individual entrepreneurs. We never saw a *maquereau* (pimp). But if they did have one, he had to be tougher than his ladies.

The greatest activity at Les Halles started in the middle of the night and ended around noon. When business was over, the area was littered with remnants of fruits, vegetables, meats, and other foodstuffs that were edible but not very pretty. A formal cleanup wasn't necessary because the *clochards*, who couldn't afford food or rent, always scavenged for their meals. We had a friend who was a student and supplemented his meal budget by stalking the pavements of Les Halles to garner a generous supply of food for absolutely nothing.

Clochards and poor students were not the only ones who took advantage of Les Halles' *embarass de richesses*. Enter the rats. Les Halles was their territory, and they gave no quarter. An army of cats tried to defeat the onslaught of rodents but retreated in shame. The rats ruled. And they rule to this day—not in Les Halles, which was moved to a suburb to make room for the Pompidou Museum, but in the *quartier* now known as the Pompidou Center. Mysterious electrical short circuits in that neighborhood defied the expertise of investigators.

Finally, to the chagrin of all concerned, it was discovered that the rats were feasting on the rubber casing around the wiring. They still are, for all I know. When the escalator stops and the lights dim, St. Gertrude, the patron saint of rats and mice, is taking her revenge on Paris for depriving her creatures of Les Halles.

The *clochards* of Paris defy all dictionary definitions. They are neither vagabonds, hobos, vagrants, beggars, nor homeless people, although they have no legal domicile and do not carry the *cartes d'iden-tité* issued to every citizen with a legal address. During the fifties, one could see *clochards* sunning themselves along the quays of the Seine, or using the river and its banks as their parlor, bedroom, and bath. They were an amiable group, whose backgrounds remained mysterious. I've heard that some *clochards* were physicians, businessmen, actors, and lawyers who preferred an anonymous life to establishment society. There were women *clochards* too, immortalized in the play *La Folle de Chaillot* by Jean Giraudoux.

One day my husband and I had an amusing encounter with a prototype of the "madwoman of Chaillot." Walking down a street on the Left Bank, we saw a motion picture company filming a scene that included *clochards* as characters. A real *clochard*, a woman of a certain age dressed in trash barrel clothes, pointed a finger at an actress in a *clochard* costume and proceeded to vilify everyone in the production for hiring actors to play *clochards* when real *clochards* would have done the job for nothing—well, not exactly nothing, just a glass or two of wine.

Sandy then offered to buy her some wine. She looked us over, decided that we were friends who could be trusted, and led us, like two dogs on a leash, to a café near Notre-Dame, whose whereabouts she asked us not to disclose. This was the *clochards'* private retreat. She introduced us to one and all, *clochards* of various ages and both sexes. My husband, in a heroic gesture, uttered the famous phrase, "Wine for everyone—all you can drink!" This was followed by a standing ovation peppered with *"Vive les Americains,"* and *"Merci!"*

I think we met every *clochard* in Paris that day. Some are immortalized in the photographs in this book. I don't know whether the secret café still exists. I promised not to reveal its location, but if you wander through the streets behind Notre-Dame, you may find it yourself.

Another neighborhood that has changed is the Marais district. The Marais is so avant-garde and chic now that I can hardly believe it once was the Jewish quarter of Paris. Rue des Rosiers, the district's main thoroughfare, was a fascinating street, with kosher restaurants and a North African Jewish café, the Lalou. This establishment served couscous and that honey-sweet confection called *brik*. Its clientele consisted mostly of unsavory characters who were black market entrepreneurs. On Saturday nights, Lami, the boss, hired a three-piece North African band and a belly dancer. She was a mature woman who wore the jingle-jangle and veils of her trade. Her enthusiastic audience man-

ern European food helped the Goldenbergs to prosper. It was my husband's suggestion that they move their establishment to larger quarters across the street. They followed his advice, and Goldenberg's was soon one of the best-known restaurants in Paris. I don't think it will ever receive four stars from the *Guide Michelin*, but that can't keep me from awarding it a gold star for its chicken soup.

I have a 1956 edition of the *Guide Michelin*, and I was amazed to read that the population of Paris at that time was 2,850,189 and that there were only nine *grande classe* restaurants and twelve with the honorable title of *élégance Parisienne*. All of those restaurants are still in existence today, and *Michelin* keeps awarding stars as though they were confetti. On a recent visit to Paris I was shocked to see a German Bierstube on Avenue George V, a McDonald's in the Lido arcades, and pizza parlors on the Champs Élysées.

I would like to say that Paris has not changed, but of course it has. What was important is still there, but the cast of characters is different. Picasso no longer buys his paints on Rue de la Grande Chaumière. Never again will I have a drink at the Coupole with Gino Severini or spend a

aged to push 100-franc notes into her cleavage and parts of her southern hemisphere. I suppose nobody looked at her face. I had no idea what she looked like until one day, when I was sitting in a train on the Métro, a simply dressed, unattractive woman greeted me as a long lost friend. I was wondering who she was when she said, "I am the belly dancer at the Lalou." She looked like somebody's grandmother, and I wouldn't be surprised if she were.

I've often wondered what happened to Wenglinski's kosher restaurant and dear Mr. Wenglinski, who joined the Resistance with his sons and hid in the woods outside of Paris for three years.

"I did it for my country," he said, "but I also got rid of my diabetes."

Goldenberg's delicatessen, now the best place in Paris for Jewish specialties, is still on Rue des Rosiers, although there is a branch on Avenue Wagram. Goldenberg's is now run by the original Mr. Goldenberg's son. We became friends with Mr. and Mrs. G while she was pregnant. They had been in Buchenwald and, when they were released, came to Paris and opened a very small shop, selling herring in the barrel, homemade sausages, and pickles. We were steady customers, and the word of mouth we spread about this oasis of East-

day with my friend Jean Cocteau. You cannot buy
an original Toulouse-Lautrec poster for $35 or find
some Berthe Morisot drawings in the flea market
for $8. I will never again eat that delectable
chateaubriand with béarnaise sauce at the little
bistro on Rue des Canettes. But the Eiffel Tower
still is the great landmark of Paris. Rodin's statue
of Balzac still stands guard in Montparnasse. And
the anonymous children in my husband's photographs from the fifties are adults now with families
of their own. Perhaps the little boy with the brief-

case will be president of France one day—or a
great actor or general or poet.

Sometimes, when I long for Paris, I light a
Gauloise cigarette. The aroma of its tobacco, the
blue haze of its smoke, and I am on the terrace of
the Deux Magots, the Coupole, or the Flore. The
sound of an accordion or the voice of Yves Mon-
tand singing *"Feuilles Mortes"* (Autumn Leaves)
evokes a period in my life that can never be
erased. I can still hear the ominous siren of the
police vans, alerting us to an impending riot. Yes,
there were riots and demonstrations and protests
for or against causes then. This is an admirable
characteristic of the Parisians, a trait that seems to
find its way from one generation to another.

I like to think of the photographs in this book as
a tribute to Paris and the spirit of individualism,
heroism, and defiance that is its citizens' birthright.

Beulah Roth
1988

The Photographs

The Venus de Milo *in the Louvre is
one of the three most famous women
in the world. Her rivals are* Mona
Lisa *and* Winged Victory.

Ramona, an Algerian transvestite,
washes the dishes for a few cafés
on Rue des Rosiers in the Marais
district.

The man at the bar chooses his drinks with care but may be fraternizing with unlikely companions. At a café in his own neighborhood, he knows and is known by everyone.

*A cellist rehearsing for a symphony
orchestra performance at the Salle
Gaveau.*

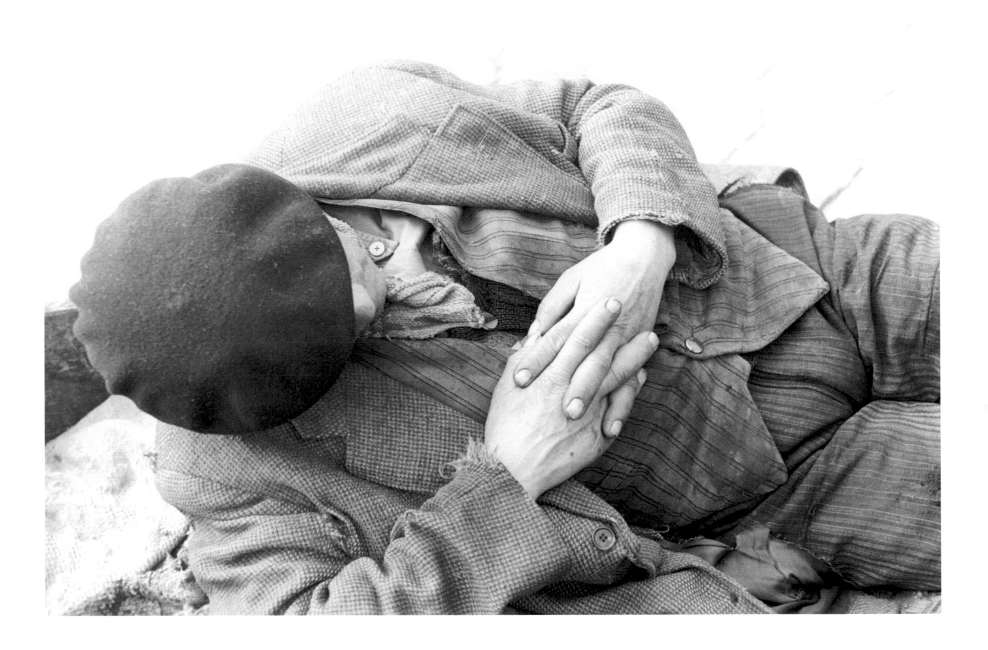

*A clochard asleep on an embankment
along the Seine.*

Clochards *use the* quais *along the Seine as parlor, bedroom, and bath.*

*The accordion and guitar contribute
to the sound of Paris. At the Café
Louisette in the Flea Market, the
repertoire of polkas, sambas, and
javas played by these musicians
makes the customers forget the cold
soup and the bad service.*

*A crowd gathers on a street
in Montmartre, attracted by the
showmanship of these song sheet
vendors.*

The photograph will become a treasured souvenir for this couple from Toulouse, celebrating their wedding anniversary in Paris.

*On Rue Guisarde, street singers with
an accordion accompanist try to sell
song sheets of popular music.*

At the base of the Eiffel Tower, she sells her ice cream to the children of Paris in the summer. In the winter she offers hot chestnuts.

A nun, anonymous in her habit, eats an ice-cream cone in the Tuileries Gardens.

*A photographer near the Eiffel Tower
takes a few minutes from his work to
discuss politics or the weather with
two gendarmes.*

*In the Tuileries Gardens, chairs that
were rented for conversation, gossip,
or intimate tête-à-têtes during the
day sit empty after the park is closed
for the night.*

Two lovers in the Tuileries have forsaken the shaded glens and wooded darkness for a bright corner of the park. This is no clandestine rendezvous but a public announcement of their devotion.

*Young boys in the Stamp Market are
already experienced philatelists.*

*The Stamp Market conducts business
every Thursday at the Rond Point.
Here collectors, browsers, novices,
and serious buyers and traders
invade the aisles of dealers who are
specialists in their fields.*

*This building on Rue de Cléry is one
room wide and five ceilings high. It
looks as fragile as a backdrop at the
Comédie Française.*

*A gendarme directs traffic on the
Place Vendôme. Behind him lies the
square where Chopin lived at number
43. Its column was destroyed in
an uprising by members of the
Commune—allegedly including
Gustave Courbet, the painter.*

In the second act of Cyrano de
Bergerac, *Rostand sets the scene in
the Shop of Ragueneau, the "Bakery
of the Poets." Ragueneau, on Rue St.
Honoré, was there in the fifties and
probably still is.*

*A bookshop on the Left Bank deals
in used volumes and engravings. The
shelves are stacked with plays, poetry,
philosophical essays, and novels, a
microcosm of French literature.*

*The late Monsieur Goldenberg stands
in front of his modest delicatessen in
the Jewish quarter of Paris.*

By the late fifties Monsieur Golden-
berg's "charcuterie orientale" had
become one of the most famous
Jewish restaurants in Paris.

*An open shutter allows some sunlight
to revive a potted plant struggling to
survive in a concierge's window.*

*A rusty lavabo in the corridor of a
tenement building on Rue Oberkampf.*

The courtyard of a building on
Rue Oberkampf.

This restaurant on Boulevard Montparnasse claims to be reserved for artists and intellectuals. Actually it is no more exclusive than the other cafés on the street whose clientele consists mainly of painters, sculptors, writers—and photographers.

*A "sandwich man" on Boulevard
des Italiens carries a motion picture
poster attached to his shoulders. The
film advertised is the French version
of* I Was a Male War Bride *with
Cary Grant.*

In the Flea Market you can learn about your future, your fortune, and your inheritance. The oracle is a disinterested parrot who plucks a pink paper with the answers from a fishbowl.

*Anything and everything is advertised
on billboards throughout Paris.*

*A delivery truck bearing the trade-
mark of a popular aperitif passes
through a street in Montparnasse
on its way to a nearby café.*

A political billboard marked with
opposing graffiti shares corner space
with an advertisement for the horse
races at every track near Paris.

The face of Dr. Pierre on the side of a building advertises his dentifrice just as it did in the nineteenth century. The bedroom windows of some tenants appear on his right eye, his upper lip, and his cravate.

*A parade watcher prefers a mirror
view of the armored divisions on
Bastille Day, Champs Élysées, 1952.*

*Using a stepladder, four women cling
to each other for an unobstructed
view of the Bastille Day parade,
Champs Élysées, 1952.*

A woman obviously prefers reading to watching the parade on the Champs Élysées, July 14, 1952.

*A demonstration against atomic
warfare was an important part
of a May Day parade, Place de
la République, 1953.*

At a May Day celebration on Place de la Bastille, Parisian children demonstrate for an end to atomic weapons and warfare.

*A group of workers in a May Day
parade advertise their political
position with a Communist salute.*

*At Place de la République on Bastille
Day, journalists, writers, editors,
and other intellectuals demonstrate
against censorship of the written
word.*

*The faces of people in a crowd on
May Day seem to reflect the pleasure
of freedom after years of horror
during the German occupation.*

This venerable couple marching in
a peace demonstration have probably
lived through two wars.

*On Boulevard Arago an elderly
couple return from the bakery with
two still-warm baguettes for their
lunch.*

At the Café Flore in Montparnasse,
afternoon tea on the terrace provides
a front row center seat to the world
passing by.

The Café Flore is a meeting place, salon, and clubhouse for young and old painters and writers in Montparnasse. From morning café au lait *to late night camomile tea, the café is a substitute for home and studio and a refuge for the lonely.*

*Bastille Day is celebrated throughout
Paris in many ways. The most typical
celebrations can be found in working-
class neighborhoods such as this one
near Place de la République.*

*In a small North African café, Lalou,
on Rue des Rosiers, the owners,
waitresses, and friends drink a toast
to Sanford and Beulah Roth, celebrating their wedding anniversary.*

An American motion picture company has turned time counterclockwise in St. Germain des Prés. Moulin Rouge actors in period costumes and the star, José Ferrer, as Toulouse-Lautrec, are seated at the Deux Magots.

Parisians are invited to taste a claret being introduced. The wine was free, but you had to bring your own glass, cup, or can to drink it.

*At an ordinary bar in an ordinary
street, a workman leaves his job to
quench his thirst with a glass of beer.*

A man dressed as a hobo confuses a
waiter but amuses the crowd in a café
during a Bastille Day celebration.

A woman waiting for the torrential
April rain to stop seeks refuge in a
friendly café on Quai d'Orsay.

Louis, the photographer's cat, is looking at the pigeons from a window in Colette's apartment on Rue de Beaujolais.

*A cat in a Montmartre grocery shop
is foraging in the window display for
an intruder. Cats all over Paris work
for their bed and board.*

A cat in the window of a café on Rue Jacob seems to know how decorative he is, sitting between two bottles of wine.

A cat who has invaded the Marché aux Oiseaux (Bird Market) feigns sleep on a cage of bullfinches, waiting for his prey—the eternal game cats play.

Two cats somewhere in Montparnasse
sleep peacefully on a windowsill.

A cat in the concierge's window on
Boulevard Arago.

A dog, wandering along the quais *of
the Seine, has just ignored the posted
prohibition.*

*The statue of Baudelaire in the
Luxembourg Gardens with a cat
paying tribute to the poet who
admired and adored felines.*

On a street in Neuilly, a young dog views a stone canine, doubtful of its intentions.

In the Bird Market, a man is trying
to see a whistling bullfinch.

*On a street near the Hôtel de Ville
(City Hall), the shops sell an extraordinary selection of fauna, from
monkeys to roosters to tropical fish.*

*These doves in an antique shop on
the Left Bank seem to be contented
with their environment.*

*In the gardens of the Palais Royal,
an American expatriate suns herself
with her pet parrot on her shoulder.*

The Cirque Médrano, one of the most famous circuses in the world, has permanent quarters in a building in Paris. To appear at the Médrano is the ultimate career goal of clowns, trapeze artists, and jugglers.

François Fratellini, one of the greatest clowns in the world, performing at the Cirque Médrano.

*The Cirque Fanni will set up a tent
almost anywhere in Paris. Overnight,
a public square becomes a circus,
to the delight of children of all ages.
Although Cirque Fanni is small,
some of its performers eventually
become stars.*

A trapeze act in the tent of the Cirque Fanni.

At the Cirque Médrano, the Maxwells,
a British balancing act, perform
before a fascinated audience.

*Watching the acrobats at the Cirque
Fanni, the audience reacts with a
spectrum of human emotions: horror,
laughter, boredom, and sympathy.*

Students at the École des Beaux-Arts
sketch from plaster casts of classic
sculptures.

*The young woman sketching in the
École des Beaux-Arts in 1952 may
now be a famous painter, an architect,
or a physicist.*

*In Montparnasse, workmen carry a
sculptor's clay figures to be cast in
bronze at a nearby foundry.*

Paysage Suisse

This sidewalk artist in Montparnasse uses the pavement as his canvas. You cannot buy his landscapes, but you can leave him a few francs in appreciation of his art.

*The bookstalls along the Seine are
an attraction for tourists, as well as
collectors and browsers. You might
find a rare first edition—or nothing
at all.*

Monsieur Michel in front of his gallery on Quai St. Michel. In the fifties, one could buy original Toulouse-Lautrec posters, Bonnard and Vuillard lithographs, and, for cat lovers, the prints of Steinlen, who loved cats too.

*Waiting for the Tour de France
to pass through his neighborhood,
a young man finds a suitable vantage
point.*

As the winners of the Tour de France
make their way to the finish line
in Paris, they pass through
the suburbs, cheered by crowds
of sports fans.

*A fiacre driver and his horse wait
patiently outside the Louvre for
a tourist to hire them.*

ACHAT
CHIFFONS, HABITS
MÉTAUX, TAPIS
MEUBLES, BIBELOTS

Vieux Papiers

Machines à Coudre

This man pushes his cart through the city streets willing to buy rags, clothing, metals, rugs, furniture, and bric-a-brac.

*Parisian housewives do most of
their marketing in street markets,
like this one in Rue Montmartre,
which specialize in fresh produce
and fruit.*

*A watercress seller places his cart
opposite the Hôtel la Louisiane,
which was used as a location in the
recent film* Round Midnight.

*It is essential to have a good eye
when browsing in the Marché aux
Puces (Flea Market). A treasure
might appear in the most unlikely
place.*

*A display of antiquities in the Marché
Paul Bert, part of Paris's famous
Flea Market.*

*The Marché aux Puces contains
an amalgam of merchandise from
the sublime to the ridiculous.
Treasures are everywhere—if you
have "the eye."*

The Marché de Ferraille (Iron Market)
is a mile-long display of rusted tools
and pipes, old stoves and toilets,
farm equipment and copper pots,
plus a smattering of antiques. This
market is an annual event for
buyers and browsers.

A little girl finds the warmth of the sun on a shadowed street in Montmartre.

*A little boy on Rue Mazarine carries
his father's briefcase with the
arrogance of a cabinet minister.*

A child amuses himself on the terrace
of the Café Select, while his parents
have an aperitif.

Sunday in the Jardin des Plantes,
the Paris zoo.

A boy holding a balloon in a public park is determined to keep it until he gets home.

A brother and sister in the Marais district are oblivious of the magnificent Renaissance doors, with elegantly carved cupids and wreaths, behind them. It is just a door to them, not a historical symbol.

*The two children assume the roles
of hero and heroine in a drama of
their own imagination.*

*Children watching a Guignol
(puppet theater) performance in a
public park react to the dramatic
adventures of Punch and Judy.*

The little girl riding the round-and-round cavalcade strives intently to hook a brass ring.

Fin

Sanford Roth Exhibitions

Los Angeles County Museum (one-man show), 1952

Mills College Art Gallery, Oakland, California (one-man show), 1952

Maryhill Museum of Fine Arts, Goldendale, Washington (one-man show), 1953

Pasadena Art Institute, Pasadena, California (one-man show), 1953

Dalzell Hatfield Gallery, Los Angeles (one-man show of photos of Utrillo), 1954

M. H. de Young Memorial Museum, San Francisco (one-man show), 1953

Chicago Art Institute (one-man show), 1954

Museum of Modern Art, New York, "The Family of Man" (participating), 1954

Al Ferro Cavallos Gallery, Rome (one-man show), 1956

Montclair Art Museum, Montclair, New Jersey, "Creative Photography" (participating), 1957

Los Angeles Art Association (one-man show), 1980

Chartwell Gallery, New York (one-man show), 1987

Los Angeles County Museum of Art, "Masters of Starlight" (participating), 1988

This book was designed by Sharon Smith, San Francisco. The text type is Bodoni Book. The display type is Choc. The type was set by Ann Flanagan Typography, Berkeley. Page mechanicals were prepared by Nancy Warner, San Francisco. Production was coordinated by Zipporah Collins, Berkeley. The text paper is 80-pound Sterling Litho Satin. The cover stock is 18-point Carolina. The endpapers are printed on 80-pound Multicolor Textured Aztec blue. The photographs are 175-line screen duotones, prepared by Arcata Graphics / Kingsport, Tennessee. Printing was done by Arcata Graphics / Kingsport. The book was bound by Horowitz / Rae, Fairfield, New Jersey.